# GOD SAID IT
## OLD TESTAMENT HEROES—1

BRADLEY BOOTH

Pacific Press® Publishing Association
Nampa, Idaho | www.pacificpress.com

Cover design by Gerald Lee Monks
Cover design resources from Marcus Mashburn
Inside design by Gerald Lee Monks
Inside illustrations by Marcus Mashburn

Copyright © 2019 by Pacific Press® Publishing Association
Printed in the United States of America
All rights reserved

The author assumes full responsibility for the accuracy of all facts and quotations as cited in this book.

Scripture quotations marked NKJV are from New King James Version®. Copyright © 1982 by Thomas Nelson. Used by permission. All rights reserved.

You can obtain additional copies of this book by calling toll-free 1-800-765-6955 or by visiting AdventistBookCenter.com.

Library of Congress Cataloging-in-Publication Data

Names: Booth, Bradley, 1957– author.
Title: God said it #4 : Old Testament heroes 1 / Bradley Booth.
Other titles: Old Testament heroes 1 | God said it number 4
Description: Nampa, Idaho : Pacific Press Publishing Association, [2019] | Audience: Ages: 6–9.
Identifiers: LCCN 2019009323 | ISBN 9780816365364 (pbk. : alk. paper)
Subjects: LCSH: Heroes in the Bible—Juvenile literature. | Bible stories, English—Old Testament.
Classification: LCC BS579.H4 B66 2019 | DDC 221.9/22—dc23 LC record available at https://lccn.loc.gov/2019009323

July 2019

# CONTENTS

Introduction ............................................................ 5

Chapter 1: Abraham and Isaac ............................................ 7

Chapter 2: Caleb and Joshua: Spies for God .................... 13

Chapter 3: Rahab: Woman of Faith ................................. 19

Chapter 4: Samson: Strongest Man to Ever Live ............ 25

## COLORING PAGES

Check out the coloring pages in the middle of this book. They are based on the featured stories and are meant to be colored in by the reader and presented as a gift to a person they appreciate. These may include

- parents,
- sisters or brothers,
- grandparents,
- aunts and uncles,
- teachers,
- neighbors, or
- friends.

# INTRODUCTION

*God Said It* introduces children to the Bible. It is designed to help children understand the importance of reading and learning from the Word of God. Our prayer is that parents, teachers, church visitors, and mentors of children everywhere use this book to reach young people for Jesus.

The Scriptures contain hundreds of stories about people trusting and obeying God, people getting to know God, and people choosing to go their own way. In the story of Abraham and Isaac, kids learn to trust God's plan—no matter what. Caleb and Joshua's story teaches about real faith in action—even when everyone is against you. Rahab's story teaches about the importance of keeping your promises. In the story of Samson, kids learn about the importance of obeying God.

*God Said It* is dedicated to God's faithful witnesses in the Bible and to all the boys and girls who read these stories. We trust that the stories on these pages will draw children to Jesus. May they choose to be faithful like the Bible heroes from long ago so that they can one day shine "like the stars forever" (Daniel 12:3, NKJV).

# ABRAHAM AND ISAAC

### THIS STORY IS FOUND IN GENESIS 21 AND 22

Abraham was one of the most famous men in the Bible. You see, God asked him to leave his fancy home in the city to ride around on a smelly camel, live in a tent, and cook over a smoky campfire. But there's more to the story.

God did not immediately tell Abraham where He wanted him to go or where he would live. He just told him He would lead him to a new country so that he could start his own tribe, who would become God's chosen people. It sounds like a wild goose chase, but Abraham had faith in God, so he obeyed.

But there was another problem. Abraham had no kids. In those days, if you had no kids, your family had no future because when you died, everyone would eventually forget about you. And that's where God stepped into the picture again. He had promised Abraham and his wife, Sarah, they would have a baby boy, but after waiting and waiting for twenty-five years, they still had no son.

Then, when Abraham and Sarah had almost given up hope, the baby was born. His birth was a surprise for everyone because by now Abraham was a hundred years old, and Sarah was ninety. It was a miracle!

They named the little boy Isaac, and everybody loved him. He probably did all the things boys love to do with their daddies, such as fishing, kicking a ball around, and listening to stories around the campfire.

And then one day when Isaac was a teenager, God spoke to Abraham and asked him to do a very strange thing. "Take Isaac to Mount Moriah and offer him as a sacrifice," He said.

A sacrifice? That seemed like a horrible thing to do. Lots of pagan nations at the time offered human sacrifices, but God had never asked His people to do anything like that. However, He had a special lesson for Abraham to learn—and for the angels who were watching to see whether Abraham would obey. It was a story people would tell for centuries to come, a story to help them understand God's plan of salvation for His people.

And did Abraham obey God? Absolutely. It was the hardest thing any father had ever been asked to do, but Abraham knew God's voice. Without delay, he took Isaac on a three-day journey to a special place called Mount Moriah.

Now, Isaac knew nothing of his father's plans. He just thought he and his father were going on a pilgrimage to offer a lamb as a sacrifice to worship the God of heaven. However, as they were walking up that last hill to the top of the mountain, Isaac said, "Father, we have brought a bundle of wood and some coals of fire for the sacrifice, but where is the lamb?"

Abraham was heartbroken. "God will provide a lamb for the sacrifice," he said with tears in his eyes.

When they got to the top of the mountain, Abraham finally told Isaac everything, and to his surprise, Isaac didn't argue. "I trust you," he must have said to his father. "God wouldn't ask us to do this if it wasn't important."

And so Abraham put the wood on the altar, laid Isaac on the wood, and gave his son a final hug. Then with shaking hands and a prayer to God, he raised the knife to heaven—but that was as far as he got. At that moment, God said, "Stop! You don't have to go through with this. It was a test, and you have passed it. There is no doubt in My mind that you love Me and will obey all My commandments."

Abraham was so relieved! His prayer had been answered, and Isaac could live after all. And wouldn't you know it? Just at that moment, Abraham noticed a ram caught in the thorny bushes nearby. His words that God would provide a lamb for the sacrifice had come true.

So they took the ram and offered it to God in worship. This showed they believed God would one day send Jesus to die for the sins of the world on Calvary. Praise God for the promise!

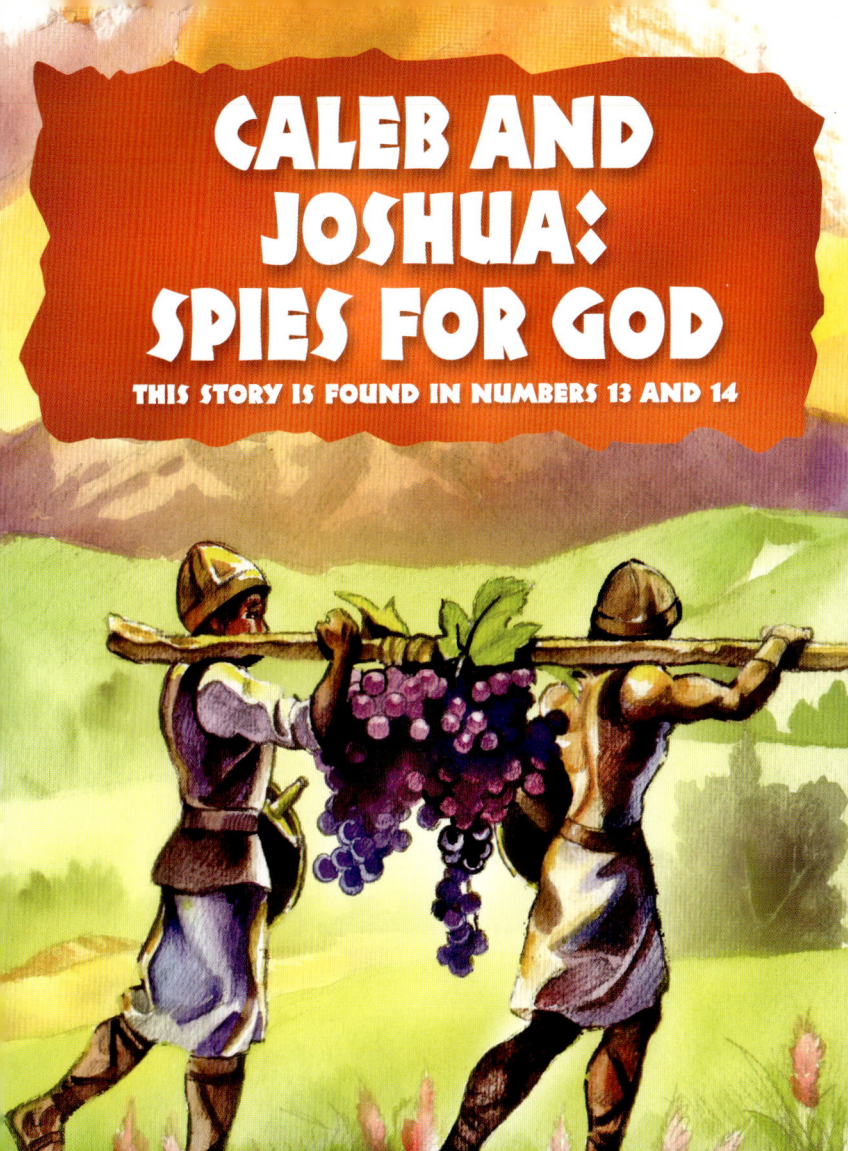

aleb and Joshua were two of the bravest men in the Bible! After escaping from Egyptian slavery and passing through the Red Sea, they helped Moses bring the tribes of Israel to the Promised Land.

Now, just two years after leaving Egypt, the Israelites were camped on the border of Canaan. To prepare to invade the land, Moses sent twelve spies to see what challenges they might face, and Caleb and Joshua were among the twelve. Off they went for forty days, marching up and down through the hills and valleys of Canaan, and what an exciting time they had!

When they got back, they had lots to tell about the amazing things they had seen. There were orchards with all kinds of fruit trees and vineyards full of grapes. There were river valleys with lots of grass for cattle and fields of golden grain overlooking the sea.

But there were other things that made the spies afraid. Fierce giants lived in cities with high walls and heavy gates. They had super weapons that the tribes of Israel did not have, such as chariots and horses and iron swords. It was all very frightening indeed!

"The giants are huge!" ten of the spies said. "We felt like grasshoppers next to them. We can't fight those guys! They would kill us as quick as a wink!"

By now all the people in the camp of Israel were scared as they listened, and everyone began to cry. "We should never have left Egypt!" they said. "We know nothing about fighting giants who are ten feet

tall! They'll squash us like bugs!"

"No! No!" Caleb and Joshua tried to calm everyone down. "We can do this! With God's help, we can conquer the land! He has promised He will help us do it!"

But the people wouldn't listen to them! They chose to believe all the scary things the ten other spies were

# ABRAHAM AND ISAAC
## GENESIS 21 AND 22

This is a gift for _____.

From _____

# CALEB AND JOSHUA: SPIES FOR GOD

**NUMBERS 13 AND 14**

This is a gift for _____.

From _____

# RAHAB: WOMAN OF FAITH
## JOSHUA 2-4, 6

This is a gift for _____.

From _____

# SAMSON: STRONGEST MAN TO EVER LIVE

**JUDGES 13-16**

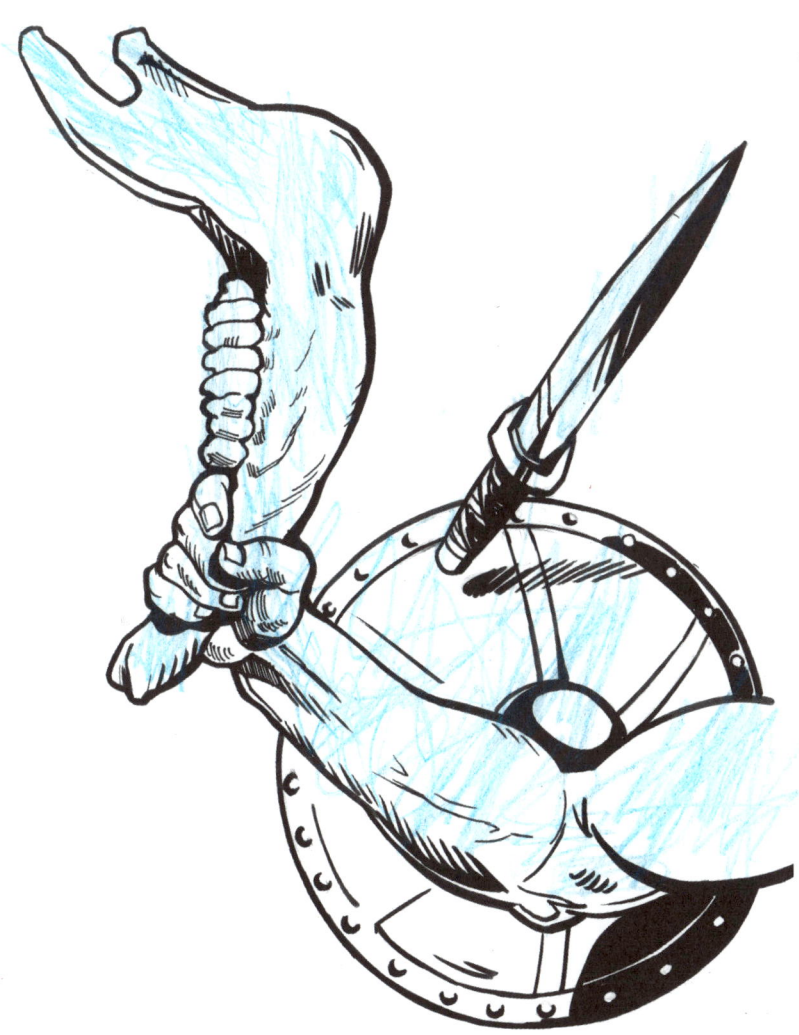

This is a gift for _____.

From _____

telling them and began to weep and wail as if they were at a funeral. "We wish we had died in the desert so that we wouldn't have to face these giants! Better yet, we should have never left Egypt in the first place! Let's choose a leader to take us back!"

Joshua and Caleb wouldn't give up. "Please, don't lose faith!" they begged. "Don't rebel against God! Have you forgotten all the amazing things He has done for us since we left Egypt just two years ago? Since He could help us escape the ten plagues and then get us through the Red Sea, He can help us fight the giants!"

However, these words just seemed to make the crowds angrier. "Kill them!" the people began shouting. "Stone them!" And they began picking up rocks to throw at Caleb and Joshua.

And that's when God stepped in. His glory blazed out from the sanctuary tabernacle, and Moses went to hear what He would say about the way everyone was acting. The people realized they had gone too far and suddenly grew quiet.

But it was too late. When Moses came out of the sanctuary, he had bad news. "You said you don't want to go into the Promised Land, and now you shall get your wish. You did not trust God when He said He would help you conquer the giants but instead believed the evil report of the ten spies. For this reason, God will not take you to the land of Canaan now as He promised. Instead, you will go back into the desert as you have asked, and there you will wander until forty years have passed—one year for each day the spies spent in the Promised Land."

The people were very sorry now for their complaining and their lack of faith, but God meant what He said, and that's exactly what happened. It wasn't until thirty-eight years later that the children of those who doubted God came again to the borders of Canaan. Only then did they get a chance to conquer the giants. True story. You can find it in your Bible.

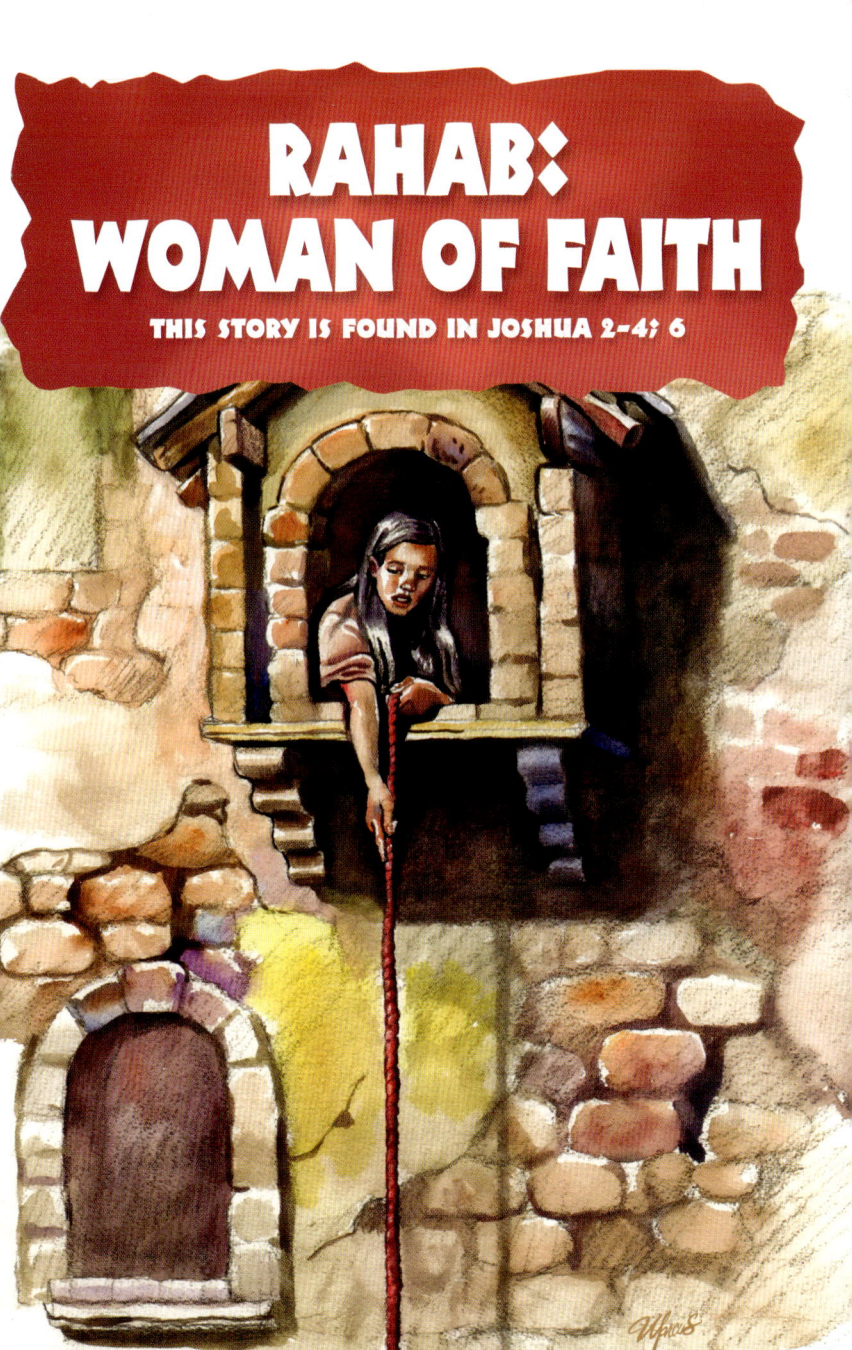

**J**ericho was the strongest, best-fortified city in the Jordan Valley, but everyone inside was terrified—and with good reason. The twelve tribes of Israel were camped just across the Jordan River to the east, ready to cross over into Canaan any day now.

Rahab was a woman who lived in Jericho. She had heard all the stories about what Jehovah, the God of Israel, had done for them, and like everyone else, she was scared.

The story gets interesting here because about this time, General Joshua sent two spies to check out the city of Jericho. They snuck into the city, trying to blend in as travelers or vendors in the market, but it didn't work. Someone must have seen them and told the king. He got suspicious and sent soldiers to find them, but the spies ran to Rahab's apartment on the city wall and asked her to help them.

She hid them on her roof under some straw—and just in time because it wasn't long before the king's soldiers came knocking on the door.

"Where are the Hebrew spies who came to your house?" they demanded.

"They were here," Rahab said. "If you hurry, you might catch them before they escape."

After the soldiers left, Rahab went up on the roof to talk with the Israelite spies. "I know Jehovah will help you conquer the land of Canaan," she said. "Your God is much more powerful than any of our gods."

"We have heard what Jehovah did to the Egyptians, and how He parted the Red Sea for you. We saw how He helped you defeat the giants across the Jordan River, and we know He will help you conquer Jericho. Our hearts are melting with fear."

"I believe in the power of your God," she added. "Now, I beg of you to save my family and me. Spare us when you conquer Jericho."

"We will promise you safety," the spies told her, "but you must not tell anyone we were here. Also, when you see our armies surround this city, bring your family inside your home and make sure they stay here. Finally, hang a red rope in your window so that we will know which house on the wall is yours."

She hung the red rope in the window, and then the spies climbed down it and snuck off into the night.

A few days later the entire Hebrew nation crossed the Jordan River when it miraculously dried up for them. This made the people inside Jericho even more afraid.

"It's another one of Jehovah's miracles!" they groaned. "Since their God can do that for them, what will He do to Jericho?"

Soldiers were sent to guard the walls and gates of Jericho, but it didn't matter much. When the Israelite army began marching around their city a few days later, the people of Jericho knew their end was near. Like everyone else, Rahab must have been afraid when she saw the huge Israelite army, but she remembered the promise the spies had made to her.

Seven days in a row the Hebrew soldiers marched around the outside wall of the city, and never did they make a sound until the seventh day. On that day they marched around the city seven times and then gave a mighty shout that hit the city like a battering ram.

There was a rumbling and crumbling, and suddenly the city wall collapsed and fell down. This allowed the armies of Israel to march in and destroy the city. But they spared Rahab and her family, who had hidden in her apartment high on the Jericho wall.

Wow! What a story! The Bible says the spies spared Rahab's life, as promised, and the lives of her family members. But God had something to do with that promise too. You see, only Rahab's home was spared. Amazing! It was as much a miracle as the parts of the wall that did fall down!

And that's important. Why? Well, Rahab was the great-great-great-grandmother of Jesus.

# SAMSON: STRONGEST MAN TO EVER LIVE

**THIS STORY IS FOUND IN JUDGES 13-16**

This amazing story from the Bible is like nothing you've ever read before! It's the story about a real superhero named Samson.

God gave Samson's parents instructions about how to raise Samson even before he was born, but the strangest command of all was that he was never to cut his hair. Wow! Even as a kid, his hair must have been really long!

When he was a grown man, Samson was asked to protect his people from their worst enemies, the Philistines. Unfortunately, he didn't like the job much and decided to party with them instead. Not surprisingly, it got him into a lot of trouble. For starters, he fell in love with one of the Philistine girls and decided to marry her. His parents begged him not to, but he did it anyway.

On the way to the wedding, he stopped to see the carcass of a lion he had killed with his bare hands, and then he made a riddle about it for the wedding guests. They couldn't solve the riddle until they pressured Samson's wife to tell them the answer, and everyone got into a big fight over the whole thing, so Samson left town. When he came back a few weeks later, he discovered his wife was now married to someone else.

That made him angry, so he caught three hundred foxes, tied burning torches between their tails, and let them loose in the grain fields of the Philistines. The Philistine soldiers were hopping mad and went in search of Samson. They found him living in a cave,

but before they could capture him, he grabbed up the jawbone of a donkey and killed a thousand of them.

Samson led Israel for twenty years. Unfortunately, that didn't stop him from going down to the cities of the Philistines to party every now and then. In Gaza he met a Philistine woman he liked and stayed with her one night. When the rulers of the city found out, they locked the iron gates so that they could capture him in the morning. But they never got their chance.

At midnight Samson grabbed the iron gates, yanked them off the city wall, and carried them to a hillside several miles away.

Next, he fell in love with a Philistine woman named Delilah, and she proved to be his greatest enemy yet. The Philistine warlords bribed her with money to find out the secret of Samson's strength, and that's exactly what she set out to do.

Three times she begged him to tell her, and three times he made up a tale about why he was so strong. The fourth time he told her the truth. "If you cut my hair, I will be as weak as anyone," he said.

And sure enough, as soon as he went to sleep that night, she called a man to come and cut off his hair. When he woke up, his supernatural strength was gone. The Philistines put him in chains, blinded him, and set him to work in prison.

Samson wished he had never told anyone the secret of his strength, but it was too late. He had been playing games with the enemy and had lost. Now he was

blind and in prison. However, his hair began to grow again.

Then on a big holiday dedicated to Dagon, the god of the Philistines, the rulers brought Samson out of prison to make fun of him. He was taken to the giant columns at the center of the temple, and while they laughed at him, he leaned on the pillars. After he prayed for God to restore his strength one last time, Samson pushed the pillars and made them topple over. This brought the temple crashing down on everyone, killing everyone underneath.

It was a sad ending to an exciting story in the Bible, but the lessons for us are important ones. We should listen to the advice of our parents, and we should choose our friends wisely. Most important, we should obey God. He knows what is best for us.

# Want to know more about what God said?

## It's easy with FREE eBooklets & Bible Guides just for you!

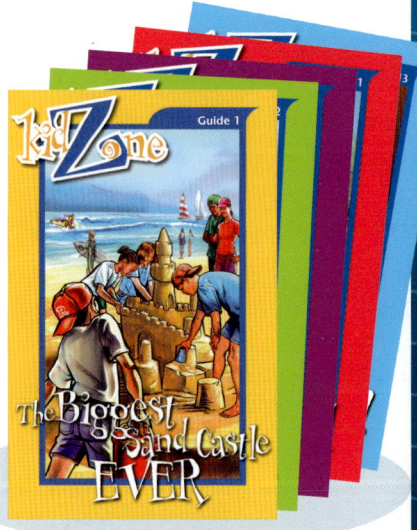

1. Go to **kidsvop.com**
2. Click on Bible Guides
3. Get started!

To receive KidZone in print, go to
**KidsBibleinfo.com/request**

**Your parents** can also learn more about what God says at **Bibleinfo.com**